NOSTALGIA
GOD'S BROKEN HEART

ERIC WILLIAM GILMOUR

SONSHIP
INTERNATIONAL

Copyright © 2016 by Eric Gilmour

Nostalgia
by Eric Gilmour

Printed in the United States of America

All rights reserved. No part of this document may be reproduced or transmitted in any form, by any means (electronic, photocopying, recording, or otherwise) without the written permission of the author.

Bible quotations are taken from *The One New Man Bible*. Copyright © 2011 by William J. Morford. Used by permission of True Potential Publishing, Inc.

Sonship International
"Living in and by the sweet empowering Presence of Jesus - seeking to bring the church into a deeper experience of God's presence in their daily lives and preaching the gospel throughout the world."
www.sonship-international.org

facebook.com/ericgilmour
instagram/sonshipintl
twitter/sonshipintl
youtube.com/ewgilmour

SONSHIP INT'L
P.O. Box 196281
Winter Springs, Fl. 32719

ISBN: 1722037334
ISBN 13: 9781722037338

"She went after other lovers and forgot Me."
—Hosea 2:13

"Their heart became proud;
therefore they forgot Me."
—Hosea 13:6

"My people have forgotten Me.
Days without number."
—Jeremiah 2:32

"You have forgotten Me."
—Ezekiel 23:35

Table of Contents

Introduction vii
Nostalgia 11
    Hosea 1:4 14
    Hosea 1:7 15
    Hosea 2:4 18
    Hosea 2:3 20
    Hosea 2:7 22
    Hosea 2:8 25
    Hosea 2:15 28
    Hosea 2:16 34
    Hosea 2:17 37
    Hosea 2:20-25 39
    Hosea 4:1 41
    Hosea 4:3 43
    Hosea 4:6 44
    Hosea 5:4-6 46
    Hosea 6:1-2 49
    Hosea 10:12 52
A Few Last Thoughts 55
About the Author 59
Additional Books by Eric Gilmour 61

Introduction

His face was made of stone and the expression on his face was deep brokenness. I knew in my spirit that his brokenhearted anguish was a fracture of the kind that only betrayed lovers know. He wasn't God; he was a human possessed with God's feelings. He, himself, in his own body bore God's emotions. By grace the Lord brought the personification of His current feelings to me through this vision and image of this prophet. In the vision I knew by intuition that this prophet of stone in front of me was Hosea.

Why was he made of stone? I am not sure. Though in other instances the Lord gave messages to prophets and told them that He would make their faces like flint (stone) to break the hardness in His people. I can only speculate that this is what God was trying to communicate to me. Hosea's burden, heart, and message would be relayed and would require a face like flint to break the hardness of His people.

Prior to this experience, the Spirit had pulled me into a series of profound illuminations through Hosea's prophetic record. Though the Lord restricted me from speaking of the things that He showed me in those days, I knew that to communicate them would one day be required of me. For over three years I waited. Then, this vision of a stone Hosea, at the turn of this year (2016), marks what I believe is a distinct disclosing of God's heart toward His people in this time.

> *Father, let these feeble letters press into the souls of Your people an image of Your broken heart over a church whose hearts have fallen in love with other things. Those who have forgotten You. Those who have forsaken the love exchange they once shared with You.*

Dear reader, many prophets have uttered God's words as divine mouthpieces but none have pictured for us God's broken heart like what we have seen in Hosea. For though others cry, "Injustice!" "Transgression!" or "Wickedness!"

Hosea's nostalgic cry is simply, "You don't love Me anymore."

Eric William Gilmour
Orlando, Florida
February 2016

Nostalgia

> "The Word of the Lord came to Hosea…in the days of Uzziah."
>
> "The Lord said to Hosea, take for yourself a wife of harlotry…for the land has committed great harlotry, departing from the Lord."
>
> — Hosea 1:1,2

In any peering into prophetic writings it is easy to note that the lives and words of the prophets are connected to the days in which they are living. In this day, God breathes into the soul of Hosea His own anguish as Hosea's personal life is turmoiled by a like agony. As the prophet receives God's words into him, he inevitably becomes God's communication to men. It was God's speaking into Hosea coupled with Hosea's obedience that brought

Hosea into union with what God was communicating of Himself to him.

It is important to understand that prophets are conduits. They are simply the means of God's message. Hosea embodies God's current heartbreak over a people who have covenanted with Him yet refuse to love Him. He has come into covenant with a woman who refuses loving-faithfulness. Though the prophets themselves personify their divine communication, Hosea's union with his holy relay is unique and arguably the clearest image of God's wounded heart, outside of Christ Himself.

Dear reader, take note. If you feel that such prophetic things are God's desire for your life, you will be united with God's feelings in the same way that Hosea was…God speaking into your soul. If God's voice isn't penetrating your heart you will never be pierced with His feelings. If you wish for a prophetic life you must share both the ecstasy of God and the agony of God. It is in the enjoyment of His ecstasy that you are enabled to receive and properly steward God's agony. In the name "Hosea" ecstasy and agony had found a home. Are you willing to house the same? If God gives Himself to us He will unite our hearts with His agony through the beatific experience of Himself.

Notice the last four words of the text. These are the words used to describe the harlotry of God's people, *"departing from the Lord."* The things that they are doing outwardly are only a fruit of a distance inwardly. To depart from the person and presence of God is the root of harlotry. If a man departs from God he loses the source of everything divine in his life: the will to obey, the sense to obey, the love for God, and even the power that comes from God.

The actions of harlotry are inevitable in a person's life whose heart has left God's presence. God must be first priority. This means that His presence is paramount. If He remains first in the heart, then harlotry can never enter it. If He is eclipsed in any form or fashion, the seed of harlotry sneaks in. The moment that we erect an idol its lifelessness begins to pass into us. This is why harlotry breeds death; man has departed from Life Himself.

Hosea 1:4

> "The Lord said to him, call his name Jezreel, for yet a little while, and I will avenge the blood of Jezreel upon the house of Jehu and will cause the Kingdom of the house of Israel to cease."
>
> *— Hosea 1:4*

Even the names of Hosea's children are indicative of the Lord's current feelings and judgment upon His people. Not only is the prophet himself an embodiment of God's communication, but it is God's desire that the prophet's family is also united with the words God has spoken into him. This is a truth I wish was more commonly understood amongst those that carry the divine sense of God's person. Our families are included in the invitation to share God's dispensing of Himself. Prophets are rare, but prophetic families are even more rare. We must allow our families into the word of the Lord.

Hosea 1:7

> "I shall have compassion on the House of Judah and will save them by the Lord their God and will not save them by bow, or by sword, or battle, or horses, or horsemen." — Hosea 1:7

The tendency of man is to look for deliverance in God's things. For instance, he looks for God's church, God's gifts, God's sovereign orchestration, or even God's Book to be the means of His deliverance in life. Hosea shows us that the Lord Himself wants to be the deliverance of His people. God doesn't want to send this or that in His stead. He doesn't want to merely give something to you as your aid. His love for man is such that His interest isn't only to deliver man but to also have man's heart. This is why God wants His very person to be the deliverance of man.

What does this mean? In giving Himself to us, we gain Him. When we gain Him we gain all. Nothing else is needed. The very fact that God Himself is the means of deliverance reveals to us that what He is delivering us from is ultimately an end and life without Him. If He Himself is the deliverance, then our destruction is His absence.

Let me say it another way. If He is deliverance, then what we are being saved from is not having Him. God is crying out through Hosea, "I want to be all to you! Let Me be all! You will find that if you receive Me you have all." God gives all, requires all, and fulfills all. He is the Only All Sufficient One. "I will…save them by the Lord their God" — not by any other means.

What specifically does it mean to receive Him as our deliverance? What does it mean for Him to deliver us? It means that His very person revealed to us and received by us through His presence and voice saves us from the destruction of not having His presence and voice. Yes, I want to emphasize this…the destruction of not having Him. The ultimate issue is the absence of God. This is why no other means can suffice. This is why a sword, a bow, a battle, horses, or horsemen mean nothing. None of these things are Him.

He could easily give means of deliverance, but His love is so great that He wants to come to us

Himself. To receive these things or anything in His stead would be to reject Him. His love is so great that to send deliverance to men outside of Himself is inconceivable to Him. What is it that we have looked for from God?

What is it that has eclipsed God Himself? Is it more power, success, money, influence, miracles, endorsements, victory, a spouse, a building? It doesn't matter what it is because without Him we only have destruction. If we lose everything but we have Him, then we have everything. If we gain everything and lose Him, we have nothing.

Hosea 2:4

> *"Let her put away her harlotries…"*
> *— Hosea 2:4*

The people have committed adultery and though the destruction of God's people is pending because man's adultery is pulling judgment upon them, God's love and faithfulness is still pulling them to Himself. The adultery of God's people is very simple to understand. Both idolatry and adultery are very different than what is commonly thought. It is not pointing to orgies, satanic practice, hatred for God, or some other obviously terrible actions alone. Such is only the fruit of a root issue. The core of the adultery and idolatry of God's people is that they are being satisfied with other things.

The reason that choosing to look for satisfaction in other things is so dangerous is simply because once a man chooses to do this he can no longer be satisfied with God. Satisfaction is not merely a perk of God's presence. It is the means by which He frees us and empowers us to be able to obey Him. A man is bound to his own lusts and self-centered cravings until he lies at the feet of Him who feeds with bread from another world.

A man has not the nutrition, health, or energy sufficient to obey God without being satisfied by eating the Christ-manna. So inevitably men stray into this and that the moment they look to find their satisfaction in something other than the person of God. As we will see in the next section, all other pursuits only destroy us both inwardly and outwardly, simply because all that man has and does was not made for anything but God (2:2).

Hosea 2:3

> "...make her as a wilderness and set her like a dry land and slay her with thirst."
> — *Hosea 2:3*

God reveals that thirst is the death sentence of spiritual adultery. Man will never be satisfied without God. Every winding road of "pleasure" is leading men away from the only true Pleasure of life and pleasurable life. I am not talking here of a life of an all-you-can-eat meat and wine cruise to the islands with an unlimited amount of spending money. As if God needs to shower us with gifts without in order to satisfy us within. I am talking about the inward bliss of His person experienced and received internally that fulfills man's soul more fully and more literally than anything that could ever be compared with physical things.

Though God can and does give us outward things richly to enjoy, He alone is our inward enjoyment. I am talking of Living Water. Men are parched and dying of thirst in their God-eclipsing pursuits. Men's souls are dry and dying from the adulterous divisions in their hearts. Our religious language, teachings, groups, music, relationships, conferences, classes, speakers, books, sermons, videos, knowledge, fasting, praying, crying, legalism, or anything else will never be worth one ounce of Living Water.

We can dance around in the river, splashing, swimming, and know all there is to know about H_2O, but it will never change the fact that no amount of outward contact with the river will ever quench the inward thirst of the soul. If a man doesn't drink (come to God for satisfaction) he will die. He will only find the shame of nakedness and the barrenness of a wilderness (2:5).

Hosea 2:7

> *"I shall go after my lovers who give me bread..."*
> — Hosea 2:7

The spiritual deception blinding the spiritual adulterer is that other things will satisfy. The adultery in the church is fueled by this tiny lie: that a man can be satisfied apart from God's presence and voice—that there is bread for the soul that did not come out of heaven; that there is drink outside of the River of Life the flows out from under the throne of God (rule of God). So because of this we have gone on and into things other than God Himself. We have exited His loving rule and sat ourselves upon the throne.

Many have survived by services, small groups, house meetings, or some other thing, but growth in the knowing of God has hardly been realized. Paul the apostle could mentor you for three whole years and John could tell you every story of the Person of Christ face-to-face, but if we believe in some small measure that there is still some satisfaction to be had outside of God, that is, His own rule through the wonderful experience of His presence and voice, then the back door is left open to walk out on Him whenever we are tempted with other things. If He has everything, there is nothing left. Jesus said, "the devil...has nothing in Me." There is no handle to grip because all has been handed over to God Himself and His will.

Once I was taken into a vision in which I saw down a long, dark alley a door with a divine light shining out from the bottom and side cracks. I knew heaven was behind this door and I was full of excitement to walk through it. When I tried to enter, it was locked. So I knocked. Out of the top of the door a little slit opened up and I could see eyes looking at me through the door. This man was smiling. I could tell from the look of His eyes that He was happy to see me. I knew it was the Lord.

He said to me, "What is the password?" Immediately I panicked because I had no idea. I thought quickly to myself, *Is it a Scripture? A name? A song?* I had no idea. I felt helpless and hopeless. I was silent for a long minute. I felt He would shut the slit and I would not be able to come in if I didn't get the password right; I felt that I should have known this. Maybe He told me and I forgot. I was deflated completely. As a grasping effort, hoping to pull on the mercy in His heart, I blurted out, "I only want You, Lord!" Immediately the door was unlocked and the sound of it knocked me out of the vision and I was back in my prayer chair.

This vision taught me so much. It is not knowledge that draws Him to us. It is not the right song or the secret mysteries that mean anything to Him. He is simply looking for that one who only wants Him. That one who finds in Him everything that they could ever desire. As long as other things are looked to we cannot see Him. Let me save you the suspense. Sex, perversions, drugs, a husband or wife, kids, money, a dream job, or even power, miracles, success, a platform, knowledge, or wonders cannot begin to scratch the surface of what it is to have Him as life and pleasure. His presence and person as the satisfaction of our souls is the sweet empowering bliss of life in God and like God.

Hosea 2:8

> "...she will not find her paths..." — Hosea 2:8

What happens to a spiritual adulterer/idolater is the inability to find her way. One thing I have run into over and over again is people in the church, both young and old, who simply have no idea what they are doing or where they are going, and they aimlessly float around, never actually bearing any fruit before the Lord. The issue in most cases is the same. Just as the eclipse of the sun darkens your way, so the eclipsing of the Son will darken your understanding.

Idolatry is an eclipse of the Son. In many instances the blindness and aimlessness of believers is an indication that something has been allowed in as an obstruction to the presence of God; something is before Him. It may be a ministry, a person, a desire for power, success, increase, lusts, money, you can fill in the blank. Anything that is placed beside Him is an idol. It is adultery.

This is more often than not the case with most of the lives that are absolutely clueless as to what they are to be in Him. For "she will not find her paths." She may seek for days, months, and even years, but her way is hidden from her until she recognizes that He Himself is the way. Many times after a long period of exhausted efforts and striving, men find the absolute end of themselves. It is here, in utter brokenness, that man has the potential to begin to sense God again.

I remember in the midst of the one of the most trying times of my life, I was dead tired in every area of life. I thought I was going to lose my wife, money was gone, we were almost living off credit, my daughter was diagnosed with an incurable disease, I was digging ditches 12-14 hours a day in the Florida sun, there was harsh oppression at my job, my heart had become lost in the world of theology, and it seemed like I didn't have a friend in the world to call. I was studying the Bible but I had lost consistent interaction with God. Due to the lack of the consistent experience of God in my life, sin was starting to creep up in my soul and it was hardening my heart. I was fatigued in every way — body, mind, emotions, and will.

In the middle of a fight with my wife, with less than $60 to my name and living in someone else's condo, I threw myself on the bed completely and totally at my wits' end. I said softly with every fiber of my being, with quiet tears streaming down my face, "God…please, help me." In that moment I felt my soul come out from under the influence of my own life and I was aware of God in all of His goodness and love. I was overwhelmed into adoration and worship. Though nothing had changed from one moment to another, everything was different. In this state of dependency He was able to resume His rule in my heart and His presence was dispensed throughout my being and I was free. Everything that is happening to you is seeking to push your soul out of dependency. If we leave dependency the means of receiving His empowering presence is forfeited.

Hosea 2:15

> "...she went after her lovers and forgot Me."
> — Hosea 2:15

Here is the definition of what it is to forget God: to seek something other than Him. Men have sought many things — money, satisfaction, success, religion, peace, joy, a spouse...many things — and it is important to note that even the gaining of whatever is sought cannot compare to Him.

We play a game amongst my brothers in the Lord. It is kind of like a "Would You Rather" game. For instance, "Would you rather be endowed by God with the power of the Spirit in such a way that no sickness can stand before you? Or would you rather be so illuminated by the Spirit that you can see into any soul at any time?" Though one picks this and the other picks that, eventually we end up at the last question, "Would you rather have everything, all gifts, all abilities in the Spirit to wield at will, or His presence?"

Every time it brings things into perspective. Nothing can compare with Him. He takes the cake over all His gifts. He wins as the unchallenged victor every time. You see, He alone is worthy. He alone is wonderful. Without Him all is dead. Without His sweet presence we have nothing. Oh dear reader, whoever you are and wherever you are in your life right now, you can seek all kinds of satisfaction, but outside of Him you will never find it. "Thou oh Christ art all I want and more than all in Thee I find."

The enemy's tricks and religious games have this main goal in view: to cause the people of God, not just to lose touch with the FACT that God is the source of her satisfaction, but to lose the EXPERIENCE of God as all her satisfaction. He will even manipulate the mind to attribute the things that God has been to us, to other things. He will lie to us and tell us that it was this event or this person in your life, or this circumstance or other situation that filled your soul with satisfaction, joy, peace, provided for you, or brought things together.

The enemy will let you have everything but God. He will encourage "deeper things" or gifts of the Spirit, your own legacy, or any other thing to detour us from God as our life source. The reason is because he knows that without the reception of God's person there is no life. The problem is, shown to us through history and our own human nature, that man wants everything but God. He will do anything but obey God. He will do anything but listen to God. He will do anything but simply trust in God.

It has been proven time after time that we can cheat on God with things that God gave us. We can keep the sacrifices going, our service and our presentation to others, the religious jargon, fads, funds, and followers, and all the while have to lose the reception of His person, which is the ultimate loss of all. It is possible to be the one known and esteemed as the one who preaches "intimacy with Jesus" and all the while have totally lost the realities of which we speak. The simple truth is that it is easy to go "after other lovers" and forget Him, even in His name, with His things.

All these efforts to bombard man's soul with things and patterns of thinking and teachings and trends and movements is to get us to forget the Lord. I am not saying that everyone who participates or is involved in these things lives in spiritual adultery, but that the tendency of man is to get a fever for the newest thing and simply fall in love with a mere pipe through which the honey of heaven is flowing.

May I remind you of what was written earlier? "Here is the definition of what it is to forget God: to seek something other than Him." Forgetting the Lord is following other loves. Any other love is far inferior to the love exchange with God. Once a man looks to things, he has forgotten God. Jesus has shown us that ways and truths commonly are separated from Him who is the Life (John 14:6). Forgetting God is mentioned by Hosea over and over (4:1-3; 10-13; 5:4). Let us not mistake what God means when He says "forgotten."

Forgetting God is not when God is out of mind, but when God is not first. It is when God is stepped in front of. Do you remember when Jesus said to Peter, "Get behind me Satan. You do not have the plans of God in your mind but the plans of men"? Jesus teaches us by this statement that the plans of men step in front of the Lord, "get behind me...," and that stepping in front of the Lord is the activity of the devil (get behind Me, Satan).

When other things are sought for satisfaction we have forgotten God. We have removed our eyes from Him and can no longer see Him. We have stepped in front of Him and can no longer be led. Here is a simple phrase that would be good to memorize: "If we go ahead we are not led." Even in the midst of the assembly, right smack dab in the center of the sanctuary, we can move on without Him. This is the beauty of waiting on God; refusing to move on without Him.

Waiting is death to the human initiative, which is the root of all waywardness. This is why silence is so uncomfortable for people, because of the inward itch to do something, say something, make something happen. It is possible, and worst of all, to lead our families, churches, friends, traditions, and lives "in His way" and all the while forget Him (Hosea 2:13).

I have met many men who were hiding the bankruptcy of their souls behind theology, intellectualism, miracles, "personal holiness," traditions, "authenticity," super spirituality, and other things. There is in fact no manifest presence in their lives. They have lost the reality of intercourse of Spirit with God. They have lost the sweet love exchange and blissful interaction with God all the while forcing their own lives and their kids' lives into a lifestyle and abstinence that they have not the spiritual nourishment to in fact be.

Hosea 2:16

> "I Am will lure her and bring her into the wilderness and speak (kindly) to her heart."
>
> — *Hosea 2:16*

Though this condition of adultery and idolatry and forgetting God in men's souls destroys people's lives and ultimately breaks God's heart, God has a remedy. A remedy of love to destroy all the works wrought by our wayward hearts and to reconcile the heart of man with His heart. God's remedy for spiritual adultery, harlots, and forgetting God is wonderful.

It is solitude, silence, and the hearing of His voice. If a man's heart gets divided God doesn't say, "Get away" but, "Come away." He wants to pull you away unto Himself and whisper in your ear. In essence He is saying to the adulterous heart, "You've forgotten Me. You've forgotten the sweetness of My Voice. There are too many other voices in your life; you've become distracted. Come away, My love."

The seduction of the enemy in its most simple analysis is simply the distraction of the heart away from God's person (presence and voice). God longs for us to come to a silent place where He can have all of our attention. Whoever will not stubbornly refuse this drawing will find that the sweetness of God's voice and the attentiveness to His presence in solitude will rip the soul away from the resolute adherence to our own will and reign.

There is nothing more attractive or satisfying than the presence, voice in the person of God. This is not my opinion or my personal experience alone—it is the actual situation of a man's soul. All men where made to be mixed with God. To be empowered by Him. To be preoccupied with Him as the source of our lives.

Adultery in the believer, idolatry in the believer, and forgetting God in the believer are all issues of a distraction that has taken our attention away from His voice and presence. Attention to His presence has been replaced with attention to other voices and the rule of our own heart. So God's remedy is to come away and let His tender voice break into your soul and melt away the bondage and cords that tie us to self-rule. After He draws men to come away…

Hosea 2:17

> "she will sing there as in the days of her youth and as in the day when she came up out of the land of Egypt." — Hosea 2:17

In this phrase we have a glimpse into the divine nostalgia. God remembers the joy and freedom of His children through first love. He recalls the liberty and chorus of the soul that irrupted the day we first met Him. It is sad to note, but most believers can remember a day in which they were closer to God than they are right now. Most can recall a time when spiritual joy was real in their hearts, yet today it is no longer that way.

Maybe you remember when your Bible was flooded with marks of interest but now your phone apps have more of your attention. Maybe you used to have to pull over to the side of the road because you couldn't see through your tears of love irrupting from your soul. Do you remember when you would steal a moment away in a closet somewhere to weep tears of love to God? Maybe your heart used to ache so bad for Him that you lay upon your pillow at night with tears saying, "I long for You!"

God remembers these days and longs for them again. He will restore such a beautiful fellowship through the wilderness of silence and solitude; a time for nothing other than sitting with God in wholehearted adoration. As verse 2:17 shows us, the covenant of love will be restored and you will call Him husband again (2:18). There is nothing that can revive a man but the breath of God received into his spiritual lungs even as lifeless Adam in stillness and death was made to live through the breath of life from God's mouth.

Hosea 2:20-25

> "I will break the bow and sword...I will make them lie down. I will betroth you to me forever...You will know the Lord...I will say to those...'You are my people.' And they will say, 'You are my God.'"
> — *Hosea 2:20-25*

Take notice of these wonderful results of God's reviving life entering a man through simply coming away.

1. I will break the bow and sword. Many people struggle and fight wars they don't need to fight simply because they are not spending time in His presence receiving the empowerment and nature they need to walk pleasing to God. Many times when I rest in His presence I say to the Lord, "Precious God, hold me. Drain out my inward poison. Hold me and cause competition, comparison, lusts, greed, anger, offense, and frustration to dissolve in me. Hold me and give me love that I don't have, joy that I long for, peace that I need, self-control, patience, kindness, and all those things that You are. For God will speak peace to His people."

2. I will make them lie down. It is not an option and it is not a potential benefit; it is a promise that His voice will bring men into rest to "make them lie down." Why is rest so important? Because it is the means by which God leads. The Spirit of God gives rest and leads (Isa. 63). Being in rest means being in God's realm. God is always seated. God is always at rest. As the Great Shepherd, "He makes us lie down in green pastures" (Psalm 23). God's very person exudes rest, and His interaction and presence passes the same into us. Unrest is the warning of the Holy Ghost. Rest is the result and state of communion with God. This is the place of bridal union with God. For immediately after He says, "I will make them lie down." He says,

3. "I will betroth you to Me..." and

4. You will know the Lord. This marital consecration is the means of coming to know God. Also notice that coming into the knowing of God is the essence of "You are My people" and "You are my God."

Hosea 4:1

> "The Lord has a controversy with the inhabitants of the land because there is no…knowledge of God in the land." — Hosea 4:1

The Scripture here mentions two things that are also lacking: "truth" and "loving kindness." Then it states many things that are being done: murder, stealing, adultery, but all of these spring out of one issue: the lack of the knowing of God. If a man fails in the knowing of God everything fails. Little by little, one by one, all falls down without the sustaining knowing of God; the presence and voice of the Lord in fellowship that causes a man to come to know God personally.

Other translations name unfaithfulness and lack of kindness as fruit of the lack of the knowledge of God (4:1). The ultimate case God has stated against His people is that they do not know Him. I wish I could install this understanding into every heart; all of the ills of mankind have one root: we do not know God. It is important to note that everything stems from here. The man who is not faithful does not know God. The man of sin does not know God. Knowing God increases as we live a life of receiving Him as enjoyment and empowerment.

Hosea 4:3

> "The land will mourn because of sin."
> — *Hosea 4:3*

Even the earth responds when men sow their sins into the sand. The reaping of destruction because of sin isn't just in an individual's life but also in the land in which he lives. Much of the way that God seems to judge sin is simply the result of the earth spewing the sins of men back at them. All of creation is groaning for the redemption of the sons of God.

Hosea 4:6

> "My people are destroyed for…lack of knowledge. Because you have rejected knowledge I will reject you. You will not be a priest to me."
> — Hosea 4:6

Reiterating to the end of time wouldn't be an over exhausting of the fact that destruction follows the lack of the knowledge of God. If we do come to know Him through the subjection of our lives, living in His presence, and receiving His words, we will end up suffering greatly. If we reject Him we join with those who were rejected by Him.

Priestliness is precious. It is reserved for those who are His. Priestliness is the difference between actions for God and actions unto God. A priest who is not wholly God's ceases to be a priest. He who rejects God's presence is rejected as a priest. For You cannot represent God to men without the true living knowledge of God that imparts His person into our lives.

If we reject the intimate touch of God, God will reject our ministry as a priest. Priesthood is the ministry of knowing God. Those who have left His presence (departed from Him) have "stopped heeding the voice" and have lost all satisfaction. The result of leaving Him and His voice is the loss of the ability to desire, love, obey, and serve Him as priest (4:6, 10).

Hosea 5:4-6

> "...the spirit of harlotry is in their midst and they have not known the Lord and the pride of Israel testifies to His face...He has withdrawn Himself from them...."   — Hosea 5:4-6

Though humanity itself is bent against God, there is actually a "spirit of harlotry." It is a literal supernatural influence pressing men toward fixation upon something other than God. It uses the "attractive" things: fleshly, natural, and even spiritual. The influence of this spirit is fourfold.

1. Deeds. A man's deeds turn against the commands of the Lord. Even more precise, man loses interest in his deeds being governed by God.

2. Do not know God. The target of spiritual harlotry is experiencing and knowing God personally, "...the spirit of harlotry is in their midst... they have not known the Lord." All of its efforts have this end in view: to block your living interaction with the person of God, which is the means by which we come to know Him personally.

3. Pride. The spirit of harlotry is fueled by pride. Arrogance permeates a man's theology, mind-sets, and life. Whether it is hyper-religious, hyper-theological, or hyper-anything, for the devil wants to settle us upon any ground by the bull's-eye.

4. Will not return to God. Men become stubborn. I have seen this over and over. A literally astounding stubbornness. A resolute and almost fierce adherence to one's own will. Have you gazed into a brother's eyes and seen this before? He who used to love and serve God with the utmost intensity or fervency or maybe even depth of wisdom and understanding has now a stone-cold face against God's living, flowing, experiential voice and presence? I have, and in that very moment it is clear as day that it has a supernatural power involved in it.

The Lord withdraws from harlotry (5:6). If we will not withdraw *with* Him we will soon withdraw *from* Him. And since a man has lost the reality of God in his life through other lovers and departing from His presence and voice, he becomes devoted to man's commands. He inevitably trusts in man to deliver him (5:11, 13).

If harlotry continues, God's heart is broken. God has longed to draw His people to Himself, and as they respond with stubbornness they are broken beyond remedy. There is no remedy for man if he will not come away. Man must acknowledge his guilt and seek His face. And in the case of hard hearts and stubborn souls, God's mercy brings affliction. For affliction has the potential to humble a man and cause him to seek God (5:15).

Hosea 6:1-2

> "Come! We will return to the Lord...He will heal us...He will revive us. Then we will know, if we follow on to know the Lord...He will come to us like the rain." — Hosea 6:1-2

The goal of repentance is to live our lives in His presence. Having His presence is our healing, for every wound was inflicted as a result of the loss of His nearness. His presence will bring life where there was death. The presence of the Lord through repentance not only heals and revives us — He is the ultimate healer and the essence of revival — but is the state in which we can go on to know the Lord.

In layman's terms, living a life of repentance is the only way He can preserve us with Him that we might, through time, come to know Him. The purpose and heart of repentance is the pursuit of living our lives in His presence — to know Him. If we seek Him we will find Him, certain as the dawn. He comes like rain from above, watering and nourishing the earth, bringing forth effortless fruit.

God breaks men through those who bear His words, "I have hewn them by My prophets. I have slain them by the words of My mouth." Prophets have become one with the weight of God's presence that God's words have enough weight through them to break men down. I remember hearing Leonard Ravenhill say, "You say that you would like to meet a prophet. Well you may want to see one but not hear him because he will leave blisters on your soul."

Hosea's flaming accusation and simultaneous invitation to God's people is tied together with the fact that He desires loyalty and knowing Him far greater than sacrifices and religious duties. Though many had "turned back to God" it was partial, "They cry out to God and turn, but not complete." What a plague amongst us today. Altars are pack with partial hearts. Man must be informed that a fire only falls on a whole sacrifice. Partiality never unlocks reality. Men must turn their backs on all other loves.

I remember being at a wedding and the minister said a phrase that touched my heart, "…forsaking all others, keeping only to thee." This is the undivided heart. Not adding God to moral resolve but literally seeking to dissolve into Him through the voluntary relinquishing of all things over to Him. Oswald Chambers once wrote, "The only right a Christian has is the right to give us his rights." That is an edible bread for God. Anything else is half-baked (7:8).

Hosea 10:12

> "Break up your fallow ground, for it is time to seek the Lord until He comes and teaches you righteousness." — Hosea 10:12

The command to "break up your fallow ground" is connected in this text with "seek the Lord." This teaches us that "hard ground" is a condition of prayerlessness. Where there is no prayer there is no sinking for the seed. The seed literally bounces off. In order for the seed to sink into the ground it must be soft enough to receive it. This is what breaking up fallow ground is. Seeking the Lord is evidence of tilled ground. Seeking the Lord is how the soul is primed and ready for the reception of God's words.

Notice what follows "seek the Lord" — "He comes and teaches you righteousness." The response of Christ to the seeking heart is His presence, "He comes...." The great teacher Himself, in His own presence and from His own mouth, will teach righteousness. Actually there is no other way to learn righteousness. Anyone can teach principles but Christ teaches what He is. Such teaching causes the words to drop from the brain into the blood. Our problem today, in the words of A.W. Tozer, is that we have "substituted logic for life." Or as Leonard Ravenhill once stated so brilliantly, "We mistake action for unction and commotion for creation."

See, God speaks Himself. Each time God speaks to you He is giving Himself to you. In your maturity as a Christian, you will become exactly whatever God says to you. He forms you by speaking into you. "He must lead you in the paths of righteousness" for His own name's sake. Becoming righteous unto God is a result of the words of Christ coming into you in His presence, "He comes and teaches you righteousness." Such receptivity of the word into your soul comes from having broken up the fallow ground through putting away all other things and seeking the Lord Himself.

A Few Last Thoughts

1. To refuse the Lord's presence as our rule, guidance, and empowerment is to receive another king. It is to be ruled, in most cases, by self. It is to be guided by your own desires and mind. It is to be empowered by our own life. Such things are a rejection of God, whether they are intended to be or not. Wherever He doesn't sit upon the throne as the ruler of the life, something, or someone else is (11:5).

2. One of the most astonishing things that I felt the Lord speak to me through this prophetic masterpiece was the accusation from the Lord against His people that they call to God but don't exalt Him. Simply stated, take adoration out and everything falls apart (11:8). There are countless people who pray and cry out to God for things. It seems that everyone is trying to get God to look at things instead of just looking at God. Many people go into

the closet to pray and they leave the same way that they came in, simple because they did everything but adore Him.

Adoration is the beginning, the sustaining, and the end of all things in God. Anyone can pray but God looks for those who will let go of everything else and adore Him. He thirsts for those who only want Him. Will you be that one who wants God just for God and not all the things that He can do for you? Will you come to Him with a heart of absolute abandonment to His beauty without any strings attached?

If Hosea's proclamation is condensed into one cry it is that God's heart is broken over His people whose eyes, heart, and soul have been taken by another. They have kept the practices going but lost love exchange with God. His people are in prayer, most likely selfish prayer, and they no longer have eyes for only Him.

3. Soon this passage will be fulfilled with glory — The Lord will make a sound like the roaring of a lion and His sons will come trembling from the west (11:10).

4. "Therefore turn to your God…wait on God continually" (Hosea 12:7). In light repentance and the new life we have in Christ, Jacob is referenced as one who found God and heard Him, and we are encouraged to now live a life of waiting upon God. Before we repented we went ahead of Him. Our repentance is turning from a life of going ahead of Him into a life of being behind Him; subjected to Him. This is living. This is true life. Life that is quickened by God by choosing to live a life of submission to Him through which we receive His power. Waiting pulls God's words toward us and then His Word pulls us into His life.

5. Pride can creep in when we become satisfied with one of God's gifts. Such a fixation upon something that comes from Him can cause us to forget God Himself. You can cheat on God with something God has given to you. This is a very important truth. How many have fallen in love with the ministry that God has given them? How many are mesmerized by their own supernatural gifts? How easy it is to rejoice in this or that and all the while forget the person of God as we continue on. No one will be able to tell that we have simply lost the touch of His presence in our closet and home.

Though the church in many ways has become a harlot having departed from the Lord, the good news is, no matter how far the distance, if men return to Him—God will heal their apostasy and love them freely—His anger will turn and His own person will be like dew upon them and they will blossom (14:4-5). We will be able to return to living in His shadow and we will blossom again. God Himself says, "Your fruit comes from Me" (14:7-9). God Himself longs to be our absolute source.

About the Author

Sonship International is a ministry started by Eric and Brooke Gilmour, seeking to bring the church into a deeper experience of God in their daily lives while preaching the Gospel throughout the world. Graduate of the Brownsville Revival School of Ministry, Eric conducts The School of His Presence in the United States and abroad. Eric is a conference speaker and author of the books *Burn, Union, Into the Cloud, Divine Life, Enjoying the Gospel,* and *The School of His Presence.*

ADDITIONAL BOOKS BY ERIC GILMOUR

Burn: Melting into the Image of Jesus
Union: The Thirsting Soul Satisfied in God
Into the Cloud: Becoming God's Spokesman
Enjoying the Gospel
Divine Life: Conversations on the Spiritual Life
The School of His Presence

Available on:
Amazon, Nook, Kindle, Kobo, iBooks

Made in the USA
Columbia, SC
03 November 2018